W9-AUD-395

WHAT DOES A LINEBACKER DO?

Paul Challen

PowerKiDS press.

New York

Published in 2015 by The Rosen Publishing Group, Inc.
29 East 21st Street, New York, NY 10010

Copyright © 2015 by The Rosen Publishing Group, Inc.

Produced for Rosen by BlueApple*Works* Inc.
Art Director: Tibor Choleva
Designer: Joshua Avramson
Photo Research: Jane Reid
Editor for BlueApple*Works*: Melissa McClellan
US Editor: Joshua Shadowens

Photo Credits: Cover, p. 25 Susan Leggett/Dreamstime; p. 1, 22, 28 James Boardman/Dreamstime; p. 3 Alhovik/Shutterstock, background Bruno Ferrari/Shutterstock; p. 4 Dennis Ku/Shutterstock; p. 5, 6, 7, 8, 10, 14, 15, 18, 19, 20, 21, 23, 29 Andy Cruz; p. 9 Olga Bogatyrenko/Shutterstock; p. 11 Lawrence Weslowski Jr/Dreamstime; p. 12 Alexey Stiop/Dreamstime; p. 13 Aspen Photo/Shutterstock; p. 16 Susan Leggett/Shutterstock; p. 17 Richard Paul Kane/Shutterstock; p. 24 Cynthia A. Jones/Dreamstime; p. 26 left Rick Sargeant/Dreamstime; p. 26 right, 27 bottom Scott Anderson/Dreamstime; p. 27 top Jerry Coli/Dreamstime; p. 28 left Tdoes1/Dreamstime

Library of Congress Cataloging-in-Publication Data

Challen, Paul C. (Paul Clarence), 1967–
What does a linebacker do? / by Paul Challen.
    pages cm. — (Football smarts)
Includes index.
ISBN 978-1-4777-7006-1 (library binding) — ISBN 978-1-4777-7007-8 (pbk.) —
ISBN 978-1-4777-7008-5 (6-pack)
1. Linebackers (Football)—Juvenile literature. 2. Line play (Football)—Juvenile literature.
I. Title.
GV951.2.C46 2015
796.332'23—dc23
                    2014004855

Manufactured in the United States of America

CPSIA Compliance Information: Batch #WS14PK8 For Further Information contact: Rosen Publishing, New York, New York at 1-800-237-9932

TABLE OF CONTENTS

THE FOOTBALL TEAM

Football teams have three parts: the **offense**, the **defense**, and special teams. Each part has a different job to do, and so does each player. The offense tries to score points. The defense tries to stop the **opponents** from scoring. Special teams take the field for kicking plays. No team can succeed without being strong in all areas. It takes skills such as speed, strength, and an ability to understand the game.

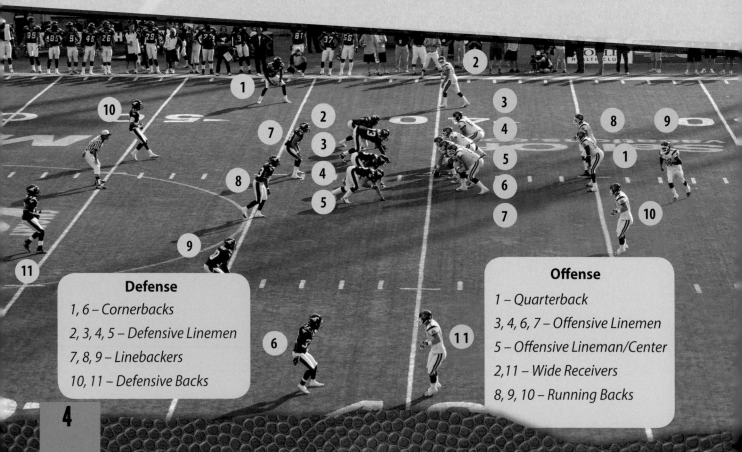

Defense
1, 6 – Cornerbacks
2, 3, 4, 5 – Defensive Linemen
7, 8, 9 – Linebackers
10, 11 – Defensive Backs

Offense
1 – Quarterback
3, 4, 6, 7 – Offensive Linemen
5 – Offensive Lineman/Center
2, 11 – Wide Receivers
8, 9, 10 – Running Backs

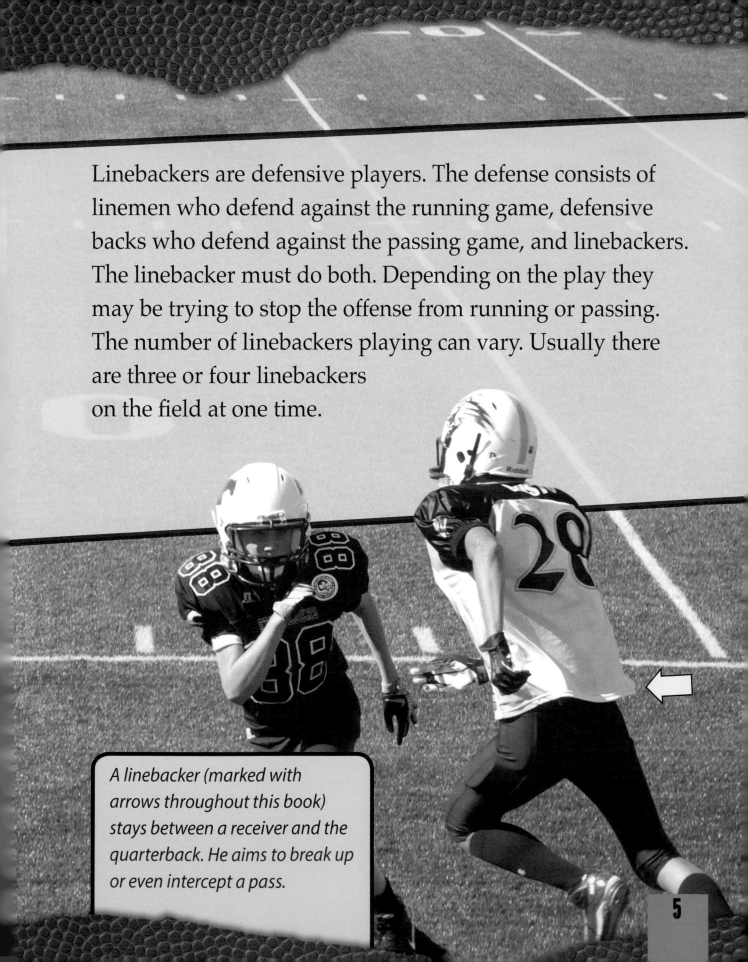

Linebackers are defensive players. The defense consists of linemen who defend against the running game, defensive backs who defend against the passing game, and linebackers. The linebacker must do both. Depending on the play they may be trying to stop the offense from running or passing. The number of linebackers playing can vary. Usually there are three or four linebackers on the field at one time.

A linebacker (marked with arrows throughout this book) stays between a receiver and the quarterback. He aims to break up or even intercept a pass.

STRATEGY

A football team's defense has the responsibility of stopping the opposing team's offense. The offensive unit tries to move the ball down the field using running or passing plays, attempting to score a **touchdown** or kick a **field goal**. Meanwhile, the defense uses tackling to stop runners. Both sides face off at the **line of scrimmage** on each play in a game.

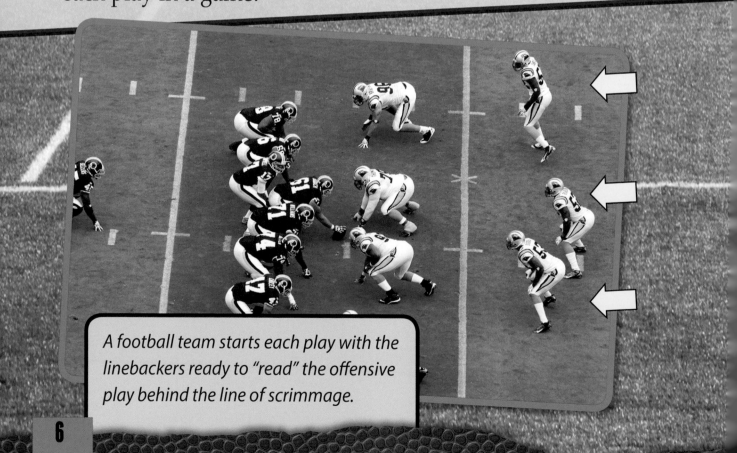

A football team starts each play with the linebackers ready to "read" the offensive play behind the line of scrimmage.

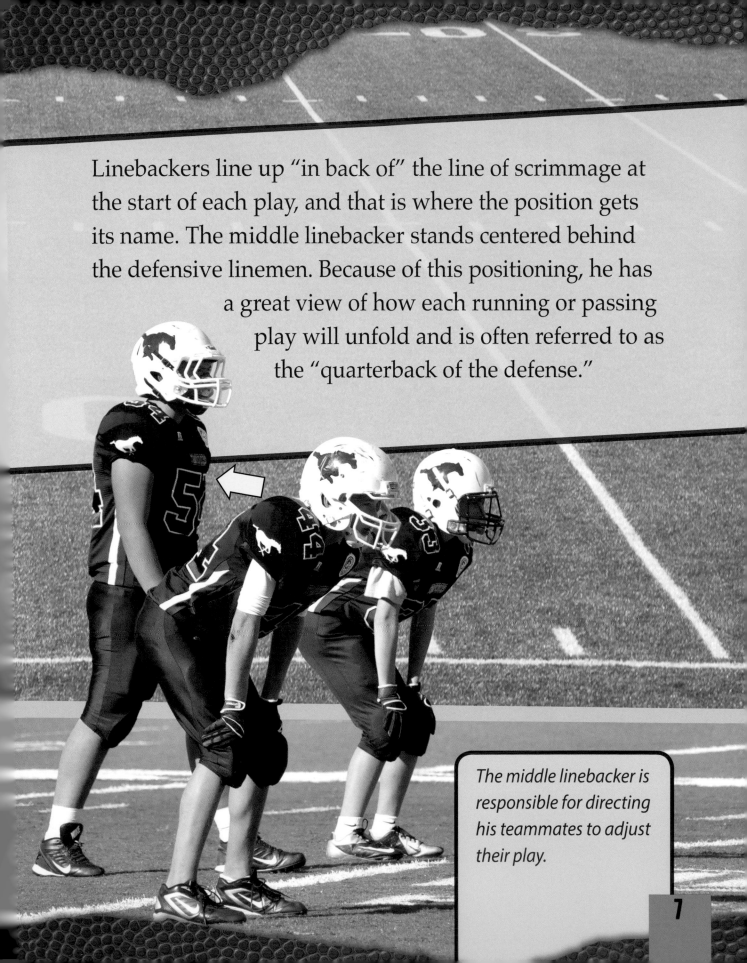

Linebackers line up "in back of" the line of scrimmage at the start of each play, and that is where the position gets its name. The middle linebacker stands centered behind the defensive linemen. Because of this positioning, he has a great view of how each running or passing play will unfold and is often referred to as the "quarterback of the defense."

The middle linebacker is responsible for directing his teammates to adjust their play.

COVERAGE

On passing plays, linebackers can use either man-to-man or zone coverage, depending on how their defensive teammates are set up. For man-to-man coverage, defensive players match up one-to-one against the offense's **receivers**. Linebackers try to stay near their assigned receivers so they can break up a passing play.

Man-to-man pass coverage is an important part of any linebacker's job. He needs to stick with a receiver to knock the ball away, make an interception, or make a tackle if the catch is made.

In zone defense, linebackers and defensive backs do not cover just one player. Instead, they protect one zone, or part, of the field. They try to keep the quarterback and receivers from completing a passing play. Each linebacker must guard any receiver who comes into his assigned zone.

Linebackers protect space in the field, which is the red triangle in this example of zone coverage.

IN THE ZONE

In zone coverage, a linebacker does not simply stand in a given zone, waiting for opponents to run into his area. Instead, when he understands what zone he is responsible for, he must sprint, back-pedal, or move side-to-side to adapt to whatever play is unfolding.

A defensive player covers his zone. It's his job to keep the receiver from getting open and catching a pass from the quarterback.

Zone coverage can be very effective if the defense executes it properly. To make it work, defensive players must get near their zone coverage areas before the **snap** of the ball. Then they can get into their assigned zone position quickly and monitor the play as it develops.

Probably the hardest thing for a linebacker in zone coverage to do is to keep his eyes on the quarterback as the play unfolds while resisting the urge to run to cover a receiver directly. The linebacker must stay in his zone and trust that his teammates are covering theirs as well.

IN OR OUT!

When a defense sets up, it uses inside and outside linebackers. As their names suggest, these defenders begin plays from scrimmage behind the offensive line either close to the ball (inside) or farther away from it (outside). Where linebackers set up depends on the defensive call. They usually line up about four yards from the line of scrimmage, but it can vary.

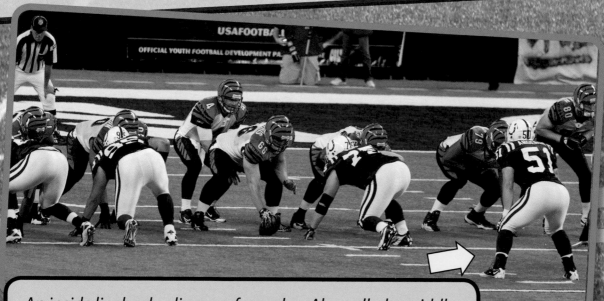

An inside linebacker lines up for a play. Also called a middle linebacker, this player is usually lined up opposite the offense's center. This lets him read the game for the defense.

Many people consider the inside linebacker to be the most important player on a team's defense, because he is the one who usually gets defensive plays from the coaches, and relays the plays to his teammates. Inside linebackers must understand the game well, and be fearless, strong, and fast.

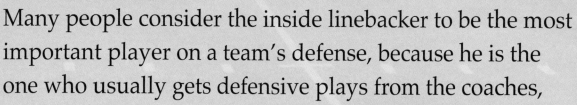

An inside linebacker has many key jobs. He controls the defense with his calls and gives directions to other players. Because he is in the middle of the defense, he follows the ball and tries to make tackles, too.

OUTSIDE LINEBACKERS

As the position's name suggests, the outside linebacker is the linebacker who sets up farthest away from the ball. His main job is to stop runners and receivers who are moving to the outside of the field, towards the sidelines. The outside linebacker also plays a big part in the defense's attempts to stop the offense by "blitzing" the quarterback—rushing in from his position to try to **sack** the quarterback behind the line of scrimmage.

Outside linebackers use speed and strength to contain runners who try to get outside.

Because of these responsibilities, the outside linebackers are often the fastest of the linebackers, and it is not unusual for them to be the smallest as well. They need great speed in going forward and agility in going side-to-side. Outside linebackers must also have the strength to knock aside **blockers**.

Linebackers have to follow the ball wherever it goes. If a ball carrier runs to one side and then switches back to the other side, the linebacker must follow quickly. Linebackers have to play sideline to sideline. They go wherever the action is.

THE RIGHT STANCE

Inside and outside linebackers get ready for the snap in similar **stances**. Both bend at the knees and crouch with their back straight. An inside linebacker stands with both feet pointed in the same direction. With his elbows against his body, he keeps his arms up and extends them in front of his body with hands open.

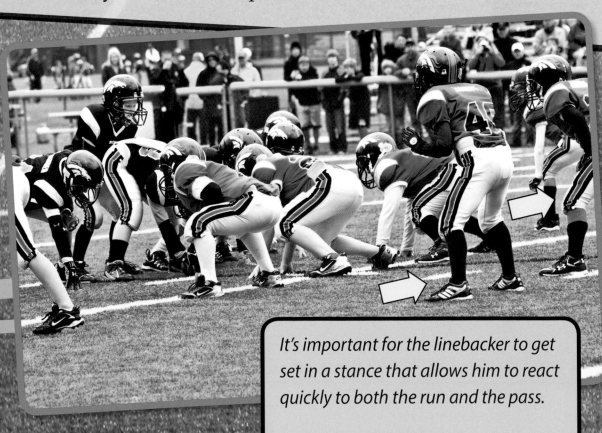

It's important for the linebacker to get set in a stance that allows him to react quickly to both the run and the pass.

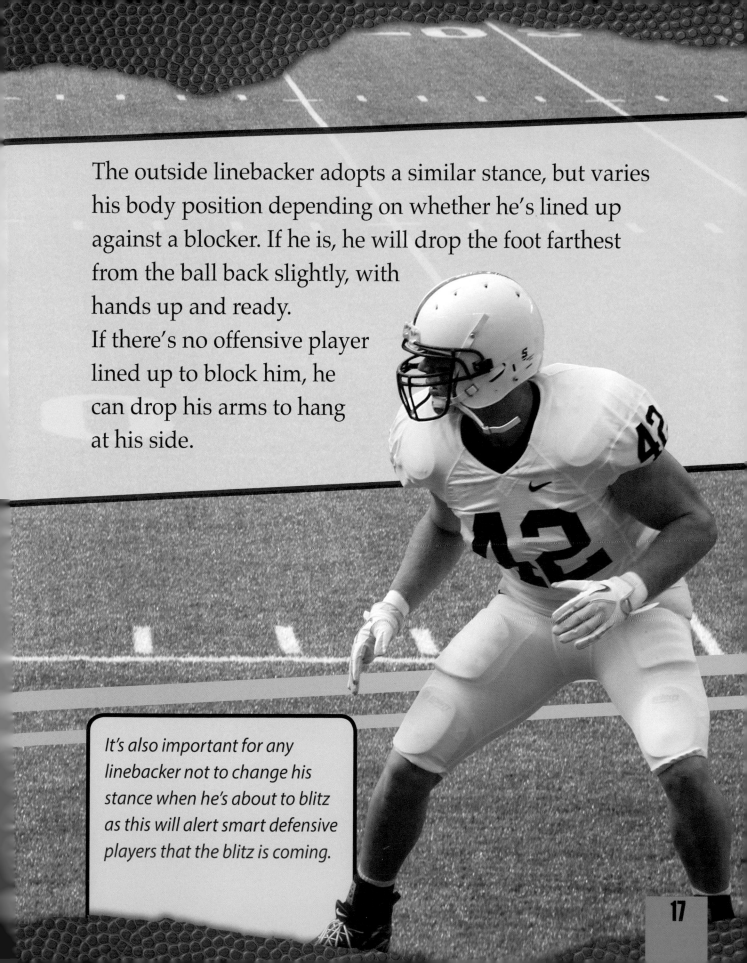

The outside linebacker adopts a similar stance, but varies his body position depending on whether he's lined up against a blocker. If he is, he will drop the foot farthest from the ball back slightly, with hands up and ready. If there's no offensive player lined up to block him, he can drop his arms to hang at his side.

It's also important for any linebacker not to change his stance when he's about to blitz as this will alert smart defensive players that the blitz is coming.

FOOTWORK

One of most important qualities a successful linebacker can have is good footwork. He has to cover so much ground on the field, and be so aware of what's going on around him that fast, agile feet are a must.

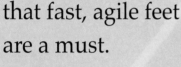

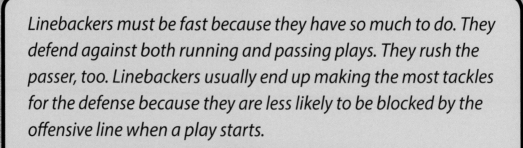

Linebackers must be fast because they have so much to do. They defend against both running and passing plays. They rush the passer, too. Linebackers usually end up making the most tackles for the defense because they are less likely to be blocked by the offensive line when a play starts.

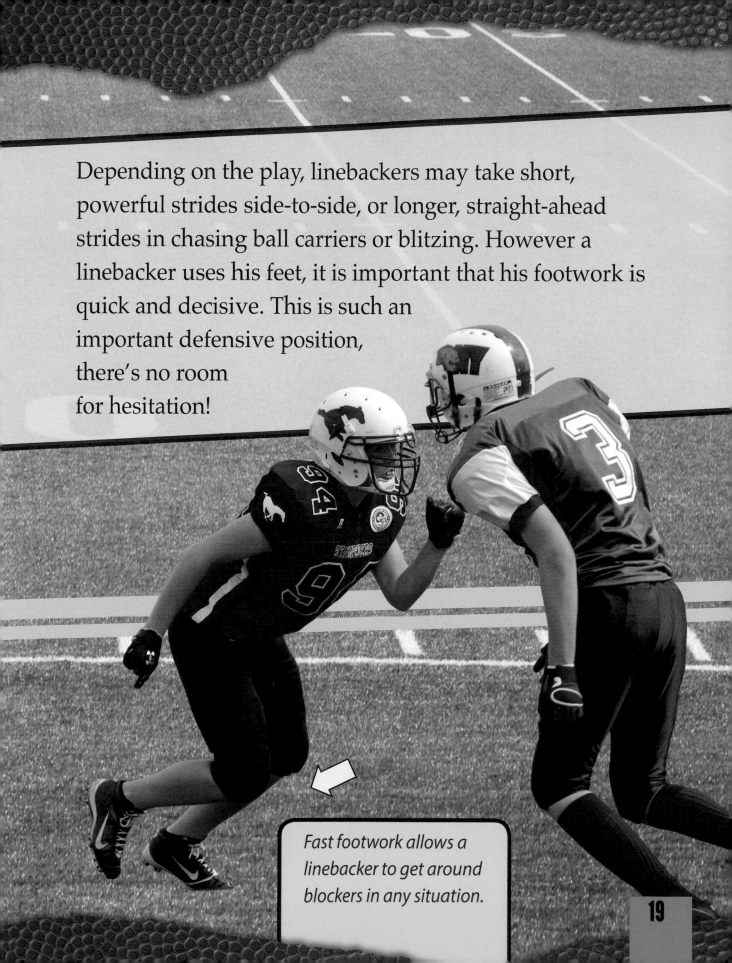

Depending on the play, linebackers may take short, powerful strides side-to-side, or longer, straight-ahead strides in chasing ball carriers or blitzing. However a linebacker uses his feet, it is important that his footwork is quick and decisive. This is such an important defensive position, there's no room for hesitation!

Fast footwork allows a linebacker to get around blockers in any situation.

BEATING BLOCKS

"Block" is the word used to describe the way an offensive player uses his body to obstruct a defensive player, usually with a push. Most blocking is done by offensive linemen. To get into position to make any kind of **tackle**, a linebacker almost always has to get around at least one block. Doing that takes strength, agility, and smarts.

Linebackers must use speed and strength to take on all kinds of blocking situations, sometimes facing multiple blockers at once.

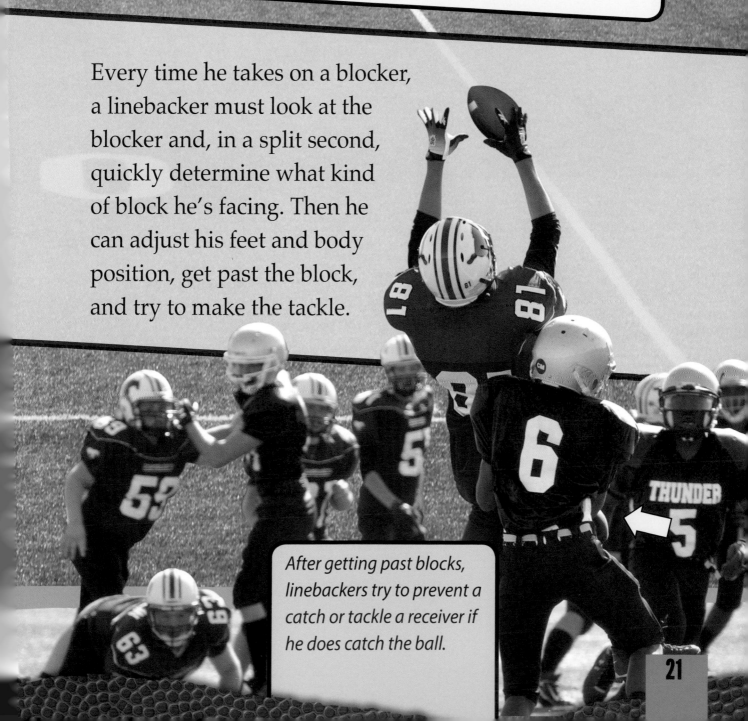

Every time he takes on a blocker, a linebacker must look at the blocker and, in a split second, quickly determine what kind of block he's facing. Then he can adjust his feet and body position, get past the block, and try to make the tackle.

After getting past blocks, linebackers try to prevent a catch or tackle a receiver if he does catch the ball.

DEEP ROUTE BLITZING

Most linebackers love to blitz! But there is a lot more to this play than simply sprinting through a hole in the offensive line and sacking the quarterback.

"Blitzing" is the name for a defensive strategy of trying to pressure the quarterback. For a blitz, at least one linebacker or defensive back tries to find a gap in the offensive line so he can rush in and tackle the quarterback. When a linebacker's blitz works to perfection, a quarterback sack is the result!

Even if the linebacker does make it past the offensive linemen, there is almost always a running back waiting to protect his quarterback. It's important to remember that even if he cannot get a sack, a blitzing linebacker can do a lot to disrupt an offense. On the other hand, leaving your usual linebacker position to blitz means you've left a gap in the defense—so there is some risk involved!

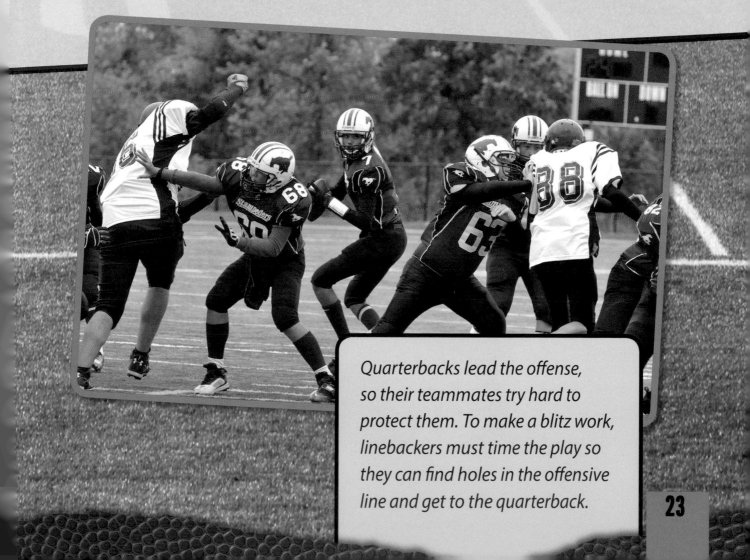

Quarterbacks lead the offense, so their teammates try hard to protect them. To make a blitz work, linebackers must time the play so they can find holes in the offensive line and get to the quarterback.

23

THE ROLE OF A COACH

Football coaches mix a team's offense and defense into a winning combination. They oversee practices and help teams get ready for games. Coaches plan a team's strategy before a game, and make important decisions during games as well. Successful coaches also know how to motivate players and teach them a love of the game.

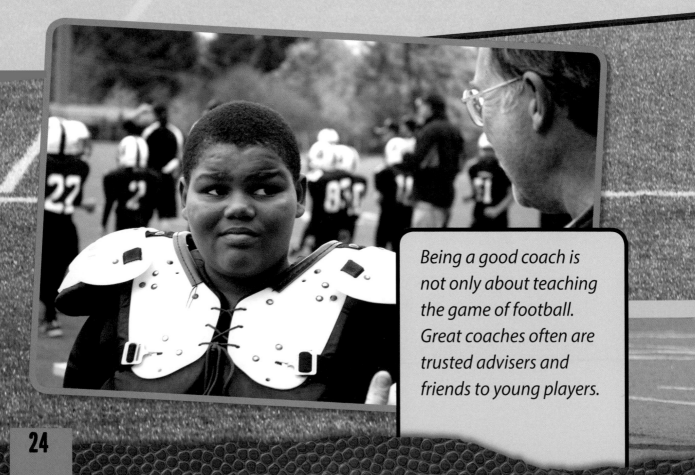

Being a good coach is not only about teaching the game of football. Great coaches often are trusted advisers and friends to young players.

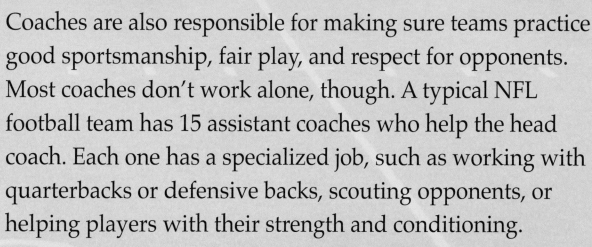

Coaches are also responsible for making sure teams practice good sportsmanship, fair play, and respect for opponents. Most coaches don't work alone, though. A typical NFL football team has 15 assistant coaches who help the head coach. Each one has a specialized job, such as working with quarterbacks or defensive backs, scouting opponents, or helping players with their strength and conditioning.

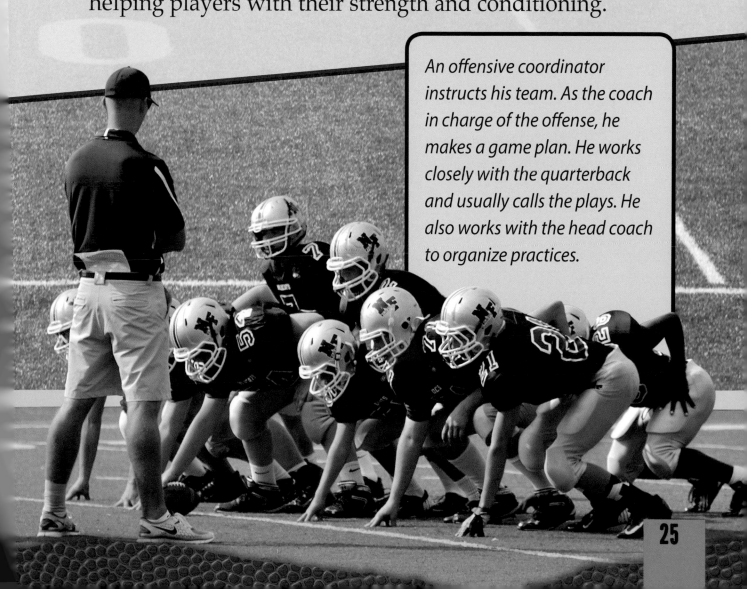

An offensive coordinator instructs his team. As the coach in charge of the offense, he makes a game plan. He works closely with the quarterback and usually calls the plays. He also works with the head coach to organize practices.

THE BEST LINEBACKERS

Many legendary linebackers have thrilled NFL fans over the years with their speed, strength, and ability to read offenses. They include Jack Lambert of the Pittsburgh Steelers, Dick Butkus of the Chicago Bears, and Tiaina Baul "Junior" Seau Jr. of the San Diego Chargers. All of these men could battle through blocks, chase down running backs, and break up enemy passing plays.

Linebacker Brian Urlacher (left) played for the Chicago Bears from 2000 to 2013. He was chosen for eight Pro Bowls and was NFL defensive player of the year in 2005.

Outside linebacker Clay Matthews (right) celebrates a sack. He has been a star pass rusher for the Green Bay Packers since 2009.

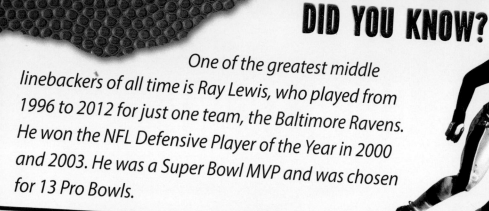

One of the greatest middle linebackers of all time is Ray Lewis, who played from 1996 to 2012 for just one team, the Baltimore Ravens. He won the NFL Defensive Player of the Year in 2000 and 2003. He was a Super Bowl MVP and was chosen for 13 Pro Bowls.

In recent years Patrick Willis and NaVorro Bowman of the San Francisco 49ers, Luke Kuechly of the Carolina Panthers, Tamba Hali of the Kansas City Chiefs, and Von Miller of the Denver Broncos have all been outstanding linebackers and big-time fan favorites.

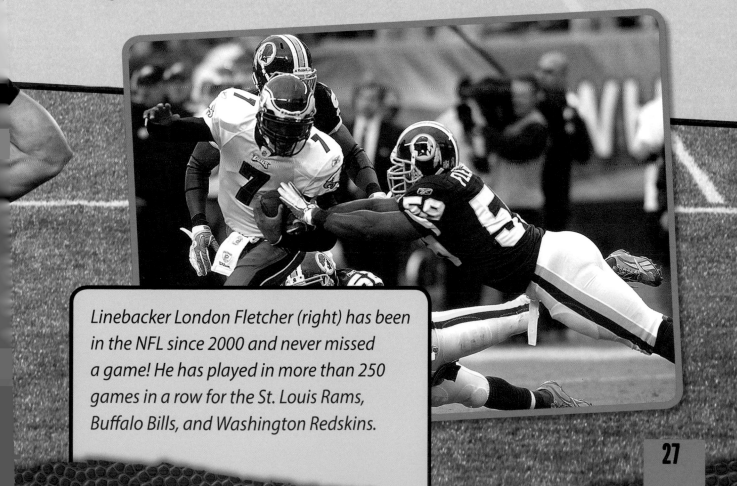

Linebacker London Fletcher (right) has been in the NFL since 2000 and never missed a game! He has played in more than 250 games in a row for the St. Louis Rams, Buffalo Bills, and Washington Redskins.

BE A GOOD SPORT

Good sportsmanship is a very important part of football. Of course, it is easy to lose your cool in the heat of a game, and react in a negative way towards the **referees**, your opponents, the fans, and even your coach. But while winning is great, respecting the rules of the game, the decisions of officials, and keeping safe are the most important ways to enjoy football!

Good sportsmanship is built on respect for your opponents, officials, and the rules of the game!

Like all sports, football has rules to make sure the game is as fair and as safe as possible for players. The rules tell what conduct is allowed and what is not. Of course, sometimes the rules are broken. This is known as a foul, and the punishment for a foul is called a penalty. Each foul has a penalty set down in the rules. When a player commits a foul, the whole team is penalized. So football players must learn and understand that playing a good, fair game is what really matters.

A player commits a holding foul by making an illegal grab on an opponent who does not have the ball. When players break rules, their team must pay a penalty. Usually it is a loss of yards, forcing the team to move backwards. Penalties are 5, 10, or 15 yards, depending on how severe the foul is. Holding is a 10-yard penalty.

GLOSSARY

blockers (BLAH-kurs) Players who are trying to stop the other team's players.

defense (DEE-fents) A group of players trying to stop points from being scored by the other team.

field goal (FEELD GOHL) A 3-point play in which the ball is kicked through the uprights of the goalpost.

line of scrimmage (LYN UV SKRIH-mij) The invisible line where the ball was last down and where the next play starts.

offense (O-fents) A group of players trying to score points for their team.

opponents (uh-POH-nents) The people or team you are competing against in a game.

receivers (rih-SEE-verz) Offensive players whose main job is to catch passes.

referees (reh-fuh-REEZ) Officials in charge of the game.

sack (SAK) To tackle the quarterback behind the line of scrimmage.

snap (SNAP) The action of the center tossing the ball between his legs to the quarterback.

stances (STANS-ez) Ways of standing.

tackle (TA-kul) To knock or throw another player to the ground.

touchdown (TUTCH-down) A play worth six points when a player carries or catches the ball in their opponents' end zone.

FOR MORE INFORMATION

FURTHER READING

Gigliotti, Jim. *Linebackers*. Game Day: Football. New York: Gareth Stevens, 2010.

Maddox, Jake. *Linebacker Block*. Team Jake Maddox. Mankato, MN: Capstone Press, 2011.

Mahaney, Ian F. *The Math of Football*. Sports Math. New York: PowerKids Press, 2012.

WEBSITES

Due to the changing nature of Internet links, PowerKids Press has developed an online list of websites related to the subject of this book. This site is updated regularly. Please use this link to access the list:

www.powerkidslinks.com/fbs/lineb/

INDEX